How to Create a Vision Board

Manifest Your Dreams with a Dreamboard in 5 Easy Steps!

Written by: Allen A. Tylor

Published under the Copyright Laws of the Library of Congress Of The United States Of America, by:

Turtle Cove Marketing
PO Box 779
Atascadero, CA 93423
Ph: (805) 268-1292

TABLE OF CONTENTS

"Your vision will become clear only when you look into your heart.
Who looks outside, dreams.
Who looks inside, awakens."
~ Carl Jung

WHAT IS A VISION BOARD?

A Vision Board (or Dream Board) is a powerful, fun and inspiring way to set and achieve personal life goals. It is a working tool that provides a physical, visual "picture" of your dreams or goals. It keeps you focused on your heart's desires. A Vision Board works with your subconscious and conscious mind to focus your mind and thoughts toward accomplishing your goals. Vision Boards create positive possibility thinking. The process of creating a vision board brings clarity to your desires and helps you manifest your life purpose.

Traditionally, Vision Boards were physical 'tools' made using a large piece of paper, poster board, or cardboard. Then pictures, words, phrases, and significant items that symbolize your dreams and goals are glued or taped on the board. However, with the advance of technology, a vision board today can be on a piece of paper, a magnetic board, a wall in your home, a PowerPoint presentation on your computer, an on-line program, a social media site such as Pinterest, or an app on your cell phone.

Vision Boards can be created by one person, by couples, with your friends, with your children, or with your co-workers and business associates. You may find that you have multiple vision boards, each one that encompasses the other and further defines your personal life goals, your family goals, your friendship goals, and your business or career goals. Or you may have a single vision board that includes each of these aspects.

"It is true that we choose our life, but it is also true that we can choose at any moment to change our path."
~ Unknown

WHY MAKE A VISION BOARD?

The reasons for making a Vision Board or dreamboard are diverse, personal and specific to each person. In general, Vision Boards help you see images of your success before you have actually achieved it. Putting your desires into tangible form, such as pictures or words, helps you get clarity on what it is that you want to create in your life. The clearer and more focused your Vision Board, the faster you will manifest those goals.

If you dream it, you can create it. Your Vision board is a visual representation that allows your conscious mind to 'see' your dreams so that your subconscious mind can create it. Vision Boards help you see images of your future success. They empower you to cultivate the dreams, excitement, and energy necessary to take action every day to bring your dreams to reality.

The universal law of attraction responds to the things and thoughts you put energy into and is a very powerful law. As a result, when you create your dream board, it is important to focus on the positive to bring more positive action into your life. Focus on what you want versus what you do not want. It is important to focus on your dreams and be careful not to censor or edit yourself. For example, if you want to meet and become friends with a famous person, put it on your board.

Some people who create dream boards focus more on what they don't want, than what they do want. As a result, they end up getting more of what they don't want rather than all the beautiful things they do want. One person constantly used "No Bankruptcy" words and pictures on her dream board each year. She could not figure out why she was always struggling for more money and on the brink of bankruptcy. When she finally realized that she was focused on not going broke, she changed her dream board to focus on being prosperous. As a result, her financial life began to immediately change. She found a better paying position and was able to start saving money for the first time in her adult life.

"Whatever the mind can conceive,

it can achieve."
~ Dr. Napoleon Hill

WHO SHOULD CREATE A VISION BOARD?

A Vision Board can be created by anyone, anywhere, any time. Everyone with a dream should create a Vision Board. People that do not have a dream should definitely create one. People who want to change or improve their lives should start with a vision board, people who want to build their families as well as people who want to transform their communities.

The teen years are often very difficult. A Vision Board is an amazing tool to use with teenagers. It assists them in seeing the long term and clarifying their goals or dreams. Teens often find that the process helps them figure out what type of career they want to have. It helps them make better choices regarding their actions, their friends and their after-school activities.

Creating a Vision Board with elementary school aged children is very rewarding - both for the child and the parent or teacher. School age children learn the basics of goal setting when they follow the Vision Board process. They learn about dreaming and looking forward to the future. It's also an excellent exercise in helping them learn about their friends and classmates.

Churches, non-profit associations, business teams, and business organization all benefit from jointly developing a Vision Board. The process unites the individuals and gets them to focus on a common goal or objective that is larger than each person. Be careful not to limit anyone's ideas and make sure that everyone participates. Share what each person learned at the end. Make multiple copies or place in a location where everyone can see it daily.

Creating a Vision Board with your friends, family and peers is an excellent way to define, focus and manifest common goals. Invite your family and friends over for a "Vision Board (or Dream Board) Party." Put out light refreshments with some fun, uplifting, inspiring music. Lay out magazines, pictures, dried flowers, etc. Explain the process to everyone. Spend the first 10 – 15 minutes in quiet meditation or relaxation while they contemplate their desires. Then everyone creates their own personal board. When everyone is finished have each person share their board and why they chose particular items.

"The future belongs to those who believe in the beauty of their dreams."
~ Eleanor Roosevelt

HOW OFTEN SHOULD YOU CREATE A VISION BOARD?

There is no hard and fast rule for how often you should create a Vision Board. Dreams grow and change over time. As you achieve your current goals, new dreams come to the surface.

For some people, creating a new Vision Board is something they do once a year. They take off the goals that they already achieved and transfer the ones not yet achieved to the new board and then add their new dreams. This way, they can see what they have accomplished over the years.

Review your previous Vision Boards at least once a year. It is interesting over time because you will begin to see a 'journal' of your life over time. You will be amazed at how much you have accomplished and achieved. You will also be surprised at the things you put on there that came true. A few years ago, I made a dream board that was mostly focused on travel. Later on, I had the opportunity to go to China although it wasn't really on my top target list. Funny, when I reviewed my old dream board – there at the top was a picture of the Great Wall. I had totally forgotten about cutting that picture or putting it on my board.

Vision boards are also fun to review with family and friends. You will be surprised at the memories that are triggered.

Some people want to achieve their dreams more quickly and as a result create a new dream board every quarter. This method gives them immediate clarification, clearer focus and instantaneous ability to correct or adjust. It is a great way to move energy into your dreams on a regular basis.

Do what feels right to you or what works best with your schedule. At a minimum, create a new Vision board at the start of each year.

"I believe that you control your destiny, that you can be what you want to be."
~ Leo Buscaglia

HOW TO CREATE A VISION BOARD

Creating a Vision Board is very simple. The hardest part is deciding what is going to go on your dream board.

This section is going to focus on creating a physical Vision Board.

Materials to have on hand:

  Glue Stick

  Tape

  Colored Markers

  Pen

  Scissors

  Magazines

  Photos

  Personal mementos

Vision Board medium (Foam-core boards, cardboard, blackboard, etc.), Power Point, On-line program or cell phone app. Decide ahead of time which medium you want to use.

Five Steps to Manifesting your Dreams

Step 1: This is the most important step as it sets the stage to achieving your dreams and goals. The more specific you are, the faster you will manifest your desires.

Find a quiet place and put on some soft music. Calm your mind either through meditation, prayer, or deep breathing. Contemplate the type of life you want to have. Let your mind wander without any restriction, editing or censoring. If you are doing a general vision board, think about the five primary areas of life and what you want in each area:

- Relationships dreams,
- Career and financial dreams,
- Spiritual dreams
- Personal and health dreams
- Physical or material dreams

You can also do a separate board for each area.

Ask yourself specific questions in each of those areas (or use the ones we prepared to get you started). Focus on what you DO want versus what you DON'T want. You can use what you don't want to assist you in identifying what you do want, but the end result must be focused on what you want. If you focus on what you don't want, you will actually create more of the same thing. For example, rather than saying "I don't want to be alone;" say, "I want to have a close, loving relationship with a person who nourishes my soul and with whom I nourish their soul."

General questions that will start you thinking in the right track are:

- What brings joy to my life?

- What are my spiritual goals?

- What do I love to do (or dislike)?

- What would I like people to remember or say about me when I'm gone?

- What types of people do I enjoy the most (or the least)?

- If I didn't have to worry about money, what would I do for a living?

- What am I most grateful for?

- What do I most regret that I can change now?

- Where do I want to live (what kind of climate)?

- How do I want my family life to be?

On the following pages you will find additional, more specific questions and a work sheet to begin writing down your thoughts and ideas. Use your own questions as well. As you work through each aspect of your life, try to mentally see the future as you are defining it. Be as specific as possible and use all your senses – what are you doing? Who's with you? What can you smell? What can you see? What do you hear? What can you feel?

Step 2: Gather items to use on your Dream Board. These items may include magazines to cut out words and pictures. It may be personal photographs you've taken or special keepsakes. Choose images that resonate with you and inspire positive feelings of joy, peace, love, passion, happiness, optimism, and so on.

Step 3: Write at the top, bottom or on the back of your Vision board your intention. For example **"This or something better now manifests for me in the appropriate time with Divine Blessings."** Write the date on your board.

Step 4: Arrange the images, words and other items on your Vision Board in a pattern that is pleasing and has meaning to you. Then glue or tape them in place. Generally, it is better to keep your Vision Board relatively organized and not too cluttered. White space is usually good because it gives 'space' for your mind to organize the vision. However, let your imagination and inspirations guide you. These are your dreams. Make it fun! Make it yours!

Step 5: Place your Vision Board in a prominent position where you can view it at least twice a day (first thing in the morning and last thing at night). When looking at it, conjure up the positive feelings and thoughts that you had when you were creating your Vision Board. Positive visual images create strong emotional energy and will keep you focused. As a result, your dreams and desires will begin to manifest and become reality.

"Your present circumstances don't determine where you can go; they merely determine where you start."
~ Nido Qubein

How to Host a Vision Board Party

If you are looking for a unique event for a bridal or baby shower, or just want to have some fun with your family and friends, hosting a Vision Board party is a great, unique way. A Vision Board party will teach you new things about your friends and family. It can also be a fun event for a business or couples party.

It is best to keep the group to 10 people or less so that it is a more intimate event. Also, make physical dreamboards versus on-line or virtual dream boards.

Gather all the items that you will need –

- Multiple pairs of scissors
- Magazines
- Multiple glue sticks
- A board for each person

Sit everyone around a table or in a circle on the floor. Put all the materials in the center of the table of circle. Put some calming music on and have everyone close their eyes and breathe deep 10 times. Walk through a meditation or relaxation technique for about five minutes. During the meditation, ask them to focus on their future life and what they want without any restrictions.

Encourage everyone to let others know what they are looking for so that each person can help each other. Set a time limit but try to have enough time so that most everyone can finish their boards. It usually takes a couple of hours.

At the end of the time period, ask each person to share their dream board and meaning behind it. It is a very moving and interesting experience. The group will be learn a lot about the others in the group and can become a strong force in helping each person achieve their goals.

"In order to carry a positive action we must develop here a positive vision."
~ Dalai Lama

How to Create a Gratitude Board

Sometimes, life gets the better of us and we forget to remember all the good things that we have in our life and all the great things that happen. A gratitude board is a great way to get back in touch with the positive events in your life as well as change negative thoughts to positive energy. Gratitude boards are an easy way to generate and maintain a positive outlook on life.

 As with the Vision Board, take a few minutes to calm your mind. Then, make a list of everything in your life that you are grateful for. Include family, friends, careers, possessions, faith, your home, and your health.

Once you have your gratitude list completed, compile pictures, words and affirmations and put them on your gratitude board. Review it on a daily basis to keep the positive energy flowing and to maintain your sense of gratitude.

"Acknowledging the good that you already have in your life is the foundation for all abundance."
~ Eckhart Tolle

DREAMS ACHIEVED, NOW WHAT?

Over the next few days, weeks, months and sometimes years, your dreams will begin to become reality. As each goal is achieved, it is important to celebrate and show gratitude for the blessings that are coming into your life. Acknowledge your achievements as they occur no matter how small. All of them are important. Gratitude allows more positive events to come into your life. You will manifest more of what you recognize, appreciate, and acknowledge.

 Then, start your next Vision Board!

"A dream is your creative vision for your life in the future."
~ Denis Waitley

VISION BOARD DREAM PLANNING WORK SHEETS

Too many people let life happen to them rather than make life work for them. Use these pages to design and create your dreams and goals. Spending quality time answering the questions about each area of your life will cause you to be in control and life to start working for you.

Look at each question and jot down the first thing that comes to your mind. Come up with your own questions. Work to eliminate all negative thinking and words such as can't, shouldn't, couldn't, and don't. Be careful not to limit yourself or place boundaries. Let your mind and your thoughts conjure up big ideas, hopes and dreams. Stay positive!

The questions are not meant to be inclusive but are designed to get you thinking so that you will come up with your own.

RELATIONSHIPS

Family

What type of family do I want to have?

What kinds of things will we do as a family?

Who will be included as part of our family?

How often will we get together?

What can I offer to make our family closer?

(Write your own questions...)

Friends

What types of friends would I like to have?

What qualities do I value in my friends?

Who would I love to meet?

What friends do I have now that I shouldn't?

What kinds of things would I like to do with friends?

(Write your own questions...)

Peers/Co-workers

What kinds of people do I want to work with?

What types of people do I admire most?

Who do I want to develop better relationships with?

What types of after work activities would I like to do with my peers?

(Write your own questions...)

CAREER AND FINANCES

What type of career do I want to have?

How much money do I want to make?

What things do I feel passionate about?

What do I want to spend the money I make?

What charities are important to me?

How large a company would I like to work for or build?

Do I want to have my own company?

What type of manager do I most like to work with?

What values and morals are important to me?

Which companies share my same values and morals?

What items do I want to buy?

(Write your own questions...)

SPIRITUAL

What beliefs do I hold?

Who has similar beliefs and can help me grow?

What do I need to do to grow spiritually?

How much time do I want to dedicate to my spiritual development?

What values are important to me?

What churches or groups have the same or similar beliefs?

What leadership qualities are important to me?

How often do I want to pray and/or meditate?

(Write your own questions...)

PERSONAL

Where would I like to travel?

Who would I love to travel with?

What activities/sports/hobbies do I like?

Where do I want to live?

What kinds of books do I want to read?

What type of home do I want to live in?

What type of furniture do I want to have?

What kind of car would I love to drive?

What 'toys' do I want to have?

(Write your own questions...)

PHYSICAL

How much do I want to weigh?

What types of food do I want to eat?

What kind of health do I want to have?

What am I willing to do to have the kind of health I want?

How much exercise do I want to get each week?

How do I want to look?

What kinds of clothes do I want to wear?

How often do I want to exercise?

(Write your own questions...)

THREE BONUS QUESTIONS

What in my life am I most grateful for?

What in my life do I have and want to celebrate?

If money was no object, what would I do with my life?

DREAM SHEET SUMMARY

Now that you have gone through all of the questions and reviewed each aspect of your life, it's time to write down your specific goals in each of the five areas.

These are the items that you are going to focus on for your dream board. Remember to be as specific and positive as possible. For example, rather than just say you want to make more money be specific as to how much money you want to make. Write, I make $100,000 or more this year.

Also remember that when you are selecting pictures, phrases or words to depict your goals, choose the ones that invoke strong, positive emotional responses.

"Things do not happen.
Things are made to happen."
~ John Kennedy

Printed in Great Britain
by Amazon

59236820R00020